Presented

to

_____

on_____

by_____

Another Tassel Is Moved

GUIDELINES FOR COLLEGE GRADUATES

LOUIS O. CALDWELL

BAKER BOOK HOUSE/GRAND RAPIDS, MICHIGAN

Copyright 1970 by Baker Book House Company
ISBN: 0-8010-2343-2
Library of Congress Card Catalog Number: 74-15631
Printed in the United States of America by Dickinson
Brothers, Inc., Grand Rapids, Mich.

Third Printing, December, 1972;

To

ALL MY FORMER STUDENTS

who have traveled the "wilderness way"
to the achievement marked by the
moving of another tassel

and especially to

PEGGY ANN BRANSCUM

who has done so much to make my own work
possible and who this year moves the tassel
for the third time and begins
to drink from the same cup

Other *Ultra Books*
by Louis O. Caldwell

*After the Tassel Is Moved: Guidelines
for High School Graduates*

The Adventure of Becoming One

When Partners Become Parents

Acknowledgements

JUDI TREAT

whose secretarial assistance reflects
the quality of her Christian commitment

MY WIFE, MAMIE; DAUGHTER, TERRI;
AND SONS, LOUIS, DAVID AND BRAD,
whose love and understanding provide
constant encouragement

Contents

. . . The Lord shall guide thee continually. . . .
— Isa. 58.11

And I said to the man who stood
at the gate of the year: Give me a light
that I may tread safely into the unknown." And
he replied: "Go out into the darkness
and put your hand into the hand of God. That
shall be to you better than light
and safer than a known way."
So I went forth and, finding the hand of God,
trod gladly into the night.
And He led me toward the hills
and the breaking of dawn in the lone East.

— Minnie Louise Haskins
in· *God Knows*

1

Joining the Ranks of the Privileged

"Better is the end of a thing than the beginning thereof."

"Much study is weariness of the flesh."

"The desire accomplished is sweet to the soul."

Possessors of the cherished sheepskin (and a truly liberal education) will recognize these quotations as those of two of the most brilliant men who have ever lived. How superbly Solomon and Paul anticipated the frame of mind of the modern college graduate!

Others have used the products of alma maters as objects for good-natured humor. Will Rogers once defined "college-bred" as a "four-year loaf." Robert Hutchins explained the reason why sheepskins are given to college graduates — "to cover up their intellectual nakedness." And, according to another, colleges become great storehouses of knowledge because freshmen bring so much in and seniors take so little out.

Add to these statements the late President Lowry's description of college graduates. They are, he believed, whether they desire to be or not, "the privileged people of their generation." Evidently, Wooster's chief administrator had a deep conviction that forty-eight months or so of living in the college environment can make a great deal of difference.

This conviction finds its support in empirical studies of students before and after their college careers. These studies tell us many changes do take place; a college environment does mold, shape and modify students. A recent study of 10,000 high school graduates revealed that those who entered college and continued on to graduation showed greater gains in independence, intellectual interests and enlightened self-awareness than those who did not attend.

But what effect does higher education have on students' values? An important study by Jacob showed that the college experience barely touches their standards of behavior, quality of judgment, sense of social responsibility, depth of understanding, and guiding beliefs. However, not all the evidence from this research is negative. Some institutions of higher learning do influence student values. But generally speaking, it appears that the impact of higher education on the value system of students cannot be called significant.

Among the more important differences between college graduates and the rest of the population are those relating to choice of marriage mate, level of marital happiness and parental success. College graduates tend to marry other college graduates, to have a lower divorce rate and to be better parents.

The ideas, interests and values of college students show remarkable enduring power. One of America's pioneers in psychology, William James, believed that

14

"outside of their own businesses, the ideas gained by men before they are twenty-five are practically the only ideas they shall have in their lives."

According to Prof. Karl Deutsch of Harvard, certain attitudes, especially those political in nature, become frozen between the ages of 15 and 25. Dr. Deutsch refers to the work of his Harvard colleague, Erik Erikson, a widely recognized authority in the field of developmental psychology. In emphasizing the relatively permanent nature of the young person's discoveries, Erikson states, "These new identifications are no longer characterized by the playfulness of childhood and the experimental zest of youth: with dire urgency they force the young individual into choices and decisions which will, with increasing immediacy, lead to commitments for life."

If the college years are the season for planting ideological seed that produces a lasting harvest, studies of another aspect of student change need national attention. Consider the study of Merit Scholars by the Center for the Study of Higher Education in Berkeley, California. These researchers discovered that 88 percent of 395 men and 91 percent of 175 women acknowledged that they had entered college with a need for religious faith. After three years of college experience, the percentage had dropped to 41 and 69 respectively.

When college graduates evaluate their education they generally call to mind their personal victories and defeats, strengths and weaknesses in faculty and curriculum. Most of them would probably find that after the evaluation was completed, they felt much the same as the writers of the following verses:

THIS IS COLLEGE

Was it in that week before Commencement,
or while I sat in the hot white sun, a prickle of sweat
under the black bachelor's gown,
or in those empty days at home?
                       Anyway,
All at once I knew a little bit about why.
I was out from under the suffocating mass of knowledge;
    there was a direction to go,
a way to do it, and I knew the way.
    I did know, had learned.
There was the door, the handle to turn, the latch to lift —
and all those years I had been finding, acquiring, filling
my pockets with keys.
Already the doors are opening. Through how many shall I
pass?[1]

The process of "finding, acquiring, filling . . . pockets
with keys" concerns personal growth. Now that you
have moved another tassel, it might be well to reflect
on your own college experiences to determine your
own growth. Consider the following kinds of growth
and try to determine how you have grown in the last
four years:

Growth in the ability to discriminate. To say that
all things are not of equal worth may sound elemen-
tary (as fundamentals have a way of sounding), but
discerning differences and choosing alternatives is not
for the naive. Hopefully, what went on during your
undergraduate days — reading, listening to over 1800
lectures, debating — generated progress in identifying
and selecting that pattern of life that is based on values
and principles that endure.

A young man just out of high school and on his way
to college was called to his pastor's study. "Promise

16

me one thing before you leave for college," said the pastor.

"Of course," replied the youth who had learned to trust his pastor, but was not a little curious.

"Promise me that you'll have the good sense of a cow."

When pressed for an explanation, the pastor continued: "Well, if you throw a cow some feed, it will be a mixture of hay and sticks. But the cow has the good sense to eat the hay and leave the sticks."

Four years later, having graduated from college, the young man returned home and informed his pastor that his advice was the wisest he had received. Using the "hay and sticks principle" should lead to an understanding and acceptance of the profound insight of a scholar of former days. He wrote:

> At present we are men looking at puzzling reflections in a mirror. The time will come when we shall see reality whole and face to face! At present all I know is a little fraction of the truth, but the time will come when I shall know it as fully as God knows me!
>
> In this life we have three great lasting qualities — faith, hope and love. But the greatest of them is love.[2]

The ability to get to the depth of things. When young William Wordsworth entered Cambridge he wrote, "My spirit was up, my thoughts full of hope." Later, he penned these lines:

> Majestic edifices should not want
> A corresponding dignity within.
> The congregating temper pervades
> Our unripe years, not wasted, should be taught.

Works which the enthusiast would perform with love.
Youth should be awed, religiously possessed
With the conviction of the power that waits
On knowledge. . . .

What does it mean to be "religiously possessed with the conviction of the power that waits on knowledge" — especially in the light of the knowledge of our time? The academic landscape is feeling the tremors of the knowledge explosion. The first doubling of knowledge occurred in 1750, the second in 1900, the third in 1950, the fourth in 1960. The fifth probably has already occurred and the sixth may be close at hand if the plot line holds.[3] Being fragmentary in nature, this knowledge cries out for two kinds of treatment. First is the microscopic view that critically analyzes; second is the macrocosmic view that brings about a synthesis. Their combination makes possible the raising and clarifying of important issues and defining of alternatives. Then the differences between the alternatives must be interpreted by relating them to a conception of life which provides the basis for intelligent living.

Growth in the pursuit of truth. Acquiring a college education should have been an experience in humility. A person who has been exposed even in a limited way to a comparison between what he knows and what there is to learn never possesses a patronizing attitude. The attitude of the truly educated has been beautifully expressed by one of the most intellectual scientists who has ever lived. "To myself," mused Sir Isaac Newton, "I seem to have been only like a boy playing on the seashore and diverting myself in now and then finding

18

a smoother pebble or a prettier shell than ordinary, whilst the great ocean of truth lay all undiscovered before me." Emerson showed the same wonderful quality when he said, "Every man I meet is my master in some points, and in that I learn from him."

The difference between mere acquisition of knowledge and the scholarly spirit is the difference between the mechanics and melody of love. Developing the love of learning enriches not only the life of the learner but those whom he will influence the rest of his years. "All things are yours" (I Cor. 3:21) is uniquely true of the college graduate who is consumed with a hunger for the truth. For him, the remainder of life's journey will be growth in the mystery of life, its paradoxes and paradises, its joys and sorrows, its growing possibilities and meaning. His quest will compel him to make all things his own. He will have a passion for understanding, for doing what he can to make necessary changes in the world and in himself, his habits, tastes and interests. Even his work will seem to him as his part of the world's work, supremely important and spiritually conceptualized.

Growth in understanding of oneself. In his commencement address to a group of graduates, Carl Sandburg said: "Young gentlemen, I think you need the spirit of prayer and humility of Abraham Lincoln who, in 'the divided house' of his day, knew what to do because he knew who he was." A great builder of another time found himself in the midst of serious problems that threatened to destroy his endeavor. After taking stock of himself, he was able to confront his enemies with this rejoinder: "Should such a man as I flee?" (Neh. 6:11). History has recorded that he did not. He stayed with his labors and completed them magnificently because he knew who he was. When Socrates said, "Know thyself," he was aware that the vital, decisive thing about a man is his estimate of himself. A formal education should teach the wisdom of Thales, who, when asked what was difficult, replied, "To know one's self."

A good deal of what we are getting at is contained in the words of the late President Lowry as he spoke to Wooster's graduating class of 1958:

> . . . this is what we give you as the last word — your own name. And you can make that, if you want to, a better thing than any diploma any college can put in your hands. You can take it out from here and set down in the big world and know what work and joy and love are till the day you die. And when you get tired and want renewal, come back here to the old ivory tower. We shall let you gripe and sign petitions and write letters to the college paper and break off your heels in the bench walks and feel young again. And strange as it may seem to you, we shall not remember your failures. We shall remember the youth and life and goodness and beauty you brought here in your time. We are very gratified for all that. We are even now grateful for what you may yet become.[4]

A distinctly Christian kind of higher education recognizes and inculcates values that abide, stresses knowledge that is fundamental and meaningfully related, inspires the pursuit of truth, and teaches the infinite worth of the individual. President Pusey of Harvard must have been thinking in these terms when he said: "It would seem to me that the finest fruit of serious learning should be the ability to speak the word God without reserve or embarrassment, certainly without adoles-

20

cent resentment; rather with some sense of communion, with reverence and with joy."

This was the spirit which Mark Hopkins tried to instill in his students at Williams College. On one occasion during his presidency, one of the students was found guilty of defacing some of the buildings and was brought into President Hopkins' office. The youth, whose family were known to be wealthy, pulled out his pocketbook and said jauntily, "Well, Doctor, what is the damage?" President Hopkins sternly instructed the young culprit to put up his pocketbook. "Tomorrow at prayers," he said, "you will make acknowledgement of your offense or you will be expelled." In commenting on the incident, the great educator said, "Rich young men come here and take that tone as if they could pay for what they get here. No student can pay for what he gets in Williams College. Can any student pay for the sacrifices of Colonel Williams and our other benefactors, for the heroic sacrifices of half-paid professors who have given their lives that young men might have, at smaller cost a liberal education? Every man here is a charity student."[5]

Robert Frost might have been thinking in a similar vein when he said that if you felt compelled to love something, you could do worse than give your heart to a college.

2

The Most Revealing Question

In my courtship and marriage class at Southern Bible College, I tell my students how they can find out the most important thing about prospective marriage mates. This great discovery can be made, according to G. K. Chesterton, by asking this question: "Do you think the universe is friendly?" Although the reaction on the part of my students often reflects something less than elation, this advice deserves pondering.

The reason why this question is of supreme importance is that it breaks through the outer layers of personality and lays bare the very core of the person. Call it a philosophy of life, a world view, metaphysical dream — whatever you may want to call it — your response to Chesterton's question reveals the explanation of the quality and course of your life. Included in the revelation are your values, goals, the secret of the pattern of your reactions and the key to what has power to motivate you.

Obviously when we begin to think along these lines

we are in the Psalmist's words "doing business in deep waters." And since this chapter began with a reference to romance it seems fitting to emphasize the need for clear thinking by recalling the young bride who stood at the altar with her hair in curlers waiting for the groom. When the astonished young man regained his composure after seeing this strange sight he asked for an explanation: "I wanted to look nice for the reception," she said.

Clear thinking about a philosophy of life should center on at least three suggestions. The first one can be exemplified by a certain man named Uncle Joe who was known for his infectious enthusiasm for life. One day a curious neighbor asked him how he managed to remain so cheerful. "Well, I'll tell you," confided Uncle Joe, "I've just learned to cooperate with the inevitable."

With that remarkable reply, Uncle Joe expressed the essence of successful, meaningful, productive living. Learning to cooperate with the inevitable is a required course in life's degree plan if we expect to "graduate." You recognize that we are dealing with what every son of Adam is trying to discover — that pattern of living that "works." And the only kind of life that works is that which is lived in accordance with the way things are. A divine purpose exists in this world. It exists for you personally and for the human family collectively. Our education is woefully incomplete unless we know that:

> Back of the loaf is the snowy flour,
> Back of the flour, the mill.
> Back of the mill are the wheat and shower
> And the sun and the Father's will.
> — Maltbie Davenport Babcock

The Divine will has been expressed in the form of law. These laws are understood as "discovered regularities" or "cause and effect relationships that are always true." These great laws sweep powerfully and majestically through the whole universe. (Because this universe is God's universe, its laws exist to serve His purpose.) The essence of reason consists in understanding the relationship of cause to effect. The reasonable life, therefore, can be lived if one seeks to discover the laws of God and then lives in accordance with them. Life becomes increasingly satisfying when we live in harmony with the mind, will and purpose of God. To oppose these laws is to be broken by them, for they are ultimately irresistible in accomplishing their divinely-appointed purpose. Sooner or later, whether drop-outs or Ph.D's, persons learn that "it's not a good world to be bad in." This was understood by that gruff old literary genius Thomas Carlyle, who, when informed that a certain lady had accepted the universe, grunted, "Egad, She'd better!"

One of the founders of modern psychiatry was Dr. Carl Jung. People from all of the civilized countries of the earth consulted with him over a period of more than thirty years. From his rich mine of experience, Dr. Jung drew this celebrated statement: "Among all my patients in the second half of life — that is to say over thirty-five — there has not been one whose problem in the last resort was not that of finding a religious outlook on life."[1]

Now if someone suspects that we are leading up to the claim that right and wrong exist independently of man he is absolutely right! Our present confusion over right and wrong exposes our dwarfed understanding of

24

the way in which we approach knowledge and truth. This problem concerning the source and nature of true knowledge leads in turn to the problem of ultimate Being. Essentially the problem turns on whether there are such things as absolutes. Another way of stating it would be to ask if there is any knowledge that is truly "authoritative." In the classic sense the only source of authority considered unimpeachable was knowledge which found its source in God. Francis Schaeffer reminds us that the first move in classical logic is the formula, "If you have A it is not non-A." This simply means that if anything is true the opposite is false. "Absolutes imply antithesis." Our present dilemma over what is right and wrong is the direct result of a large scale rejection of absolutes.

Most higher education furnishes us with an unhappy example of the modern flight away from absolute truth. Recently a retiring college president stated: "Modern educational philosophy has departed from the values of the Bible. No absolute values are any longer believed or taught by the educational establishment."[2] Yet the Aspen Institute for Humanistic Studies admitted:

> Places of higher education are, in the modern world (a world in which religion has lost its universal authority), the chief custodians and interpreters of value in society.[3]

And to show how absurd the reasoning based on relativism is, the report went on to say:

> We think it improper to impose a rigid and preconceived moral system on students, but we insist that they discover and develop their own value system.[4]

Add to these statements made in the Aspen Report the following one made by Dr. Jacqueline Grennan, President of Webster College. Speaking in a panel discussion on modern education she said:

> Only if we open up the system and let him [the student] see that there is no absolute morality, no absolute truth, but only an awful responsibility to try to find it — only then, I think, can we open up the dialogue and have the student share responsibility with us.[5]

Putting these three statements together, we come up with some remarkable double-talk: A college should interpret values, and at the same time *evaluate* religious values by denying absolute truth. Having denied the existence of absolutes, educators proceed to call upon students to engage in their discovery! No wonder that mental and moral breakdowns as well as suicides are increasing among today's college students. How much more often will we be hearing comments such as that made by one graduating senior who said, "I feel as if college has given me a wheel with the spokes missing"?

If truth cannot be absolute, it must be relative. This philosophy when expressed morally and ethically is currently named the "new morality" or "situation ethics." One of its leading proponents is Dr. Joseph T. Fletcher, former professor of social ethics at Cambridge Episcopal Theological School. He advocates modifying each of the Ten Commandments to read:

Thou shalt not kill, ordinarily.
Thou shalt not steal, ordinarily.
Thou shalt not commit adultery, ordinarily.

Advocates of the concept that truth is relative t

individual would do well to read how Socrates dealt with one of his contemporaries who held with this ancient belief. The following paraphrased dialogue between Socrates and Protagoras shows how the venerable philosopher dealt the death blow to relativism:

PROTAGORAS: Truth is relative, it is only a matter of opinion.

SOCRATES: You mean that truth is mere subjective opinion?

PROTAGORAS: Exactly. What is true for you is true for you, and what is true for me, is true for me. Truth is subjective.

SOCRATES: Do you really mean that? That my opinion is true by virtue of its being my opinion?

PROTAGORAS: Indeed I do.

SOCRATES: My opinion is: Truth is absolute, not opinion, and that you, Mr. Protagoras, are absolutely in error. Since this is my opinion, then you must grant that it is true according to your philosophy.

PROTAGORAS: You are quite correct, Socrates.[6]

A little thought leads to the realization that without an acceptance of objective truth, man cannot validly appeal to his reason. For reason performs in the service of the will, which is a function of character, and character is the ethical product of the individual's world view. "Be reasonable, see it my way" is, on the verbal level, an illustration of how ideas conveniently serve our perceptions. This same insight is found in the following:

In matters controversial
My perception's always fine.
I always see both points of view —
The one that's wrong and mine!

This relationship of reason to life-orientation was never

seen and expressed more clearly than by Christ who said, "The lamp of your body is your eye. When your eye is sound, your whole body is full of light, but when your eye is evil your whole body is full of darkness. So be very careful that your light never becomes darkness. For if your whole body is full of light, with no part of it in shadow, it will all be radiant — it will be like having a bright lamp to give you light."[7]

Once a world view is developed, the rational faculty will be in the service of metaphysical dream or vision. It becomes apparent then that logic depends upon the vision; and not the vision upon it. As Richard Weaver has pointed out, conscious reflection takes place on three levels: specific ideas about things, general beliefs or convictions, and the metaphysical dream of the world or world view. At the base of the matter is the need for a conception of creation, the nature and destiny of man that will impel him to aspire and to identify those ideals which furnish the goals for the aspiring. Christians are committed to the belief that all this is provided in the Christ-centered world view. How fortunate is that graduate who can answer the question, "Is the universe friendly?" with the words of Whittier:

> Here in the maddening maze of times
> When tossed by storm and flood
> To one fixed ground my spirit clings
> I know that God is good.

The second suggestion regarding the constructing of a workable, realistic philosophy of life is this: Take the wilderness way to wherever you want to go.

One of the most meaningful of the yearly celebrations of our Jewish friends is the Feast of Sukkos. This

28

reminds them of the wilderness wanderings. You will recall their great exodus from Egypt and their historic journey to the promised land under the direction of Moses. Geographically it was only two hundred miles from Egypt to Canaan. Allowing twenty miles per day for nomadic travel, they should have made the trek in ten days. But the journey took forty years. ". . . But God led the people about, through the way of the wilderness . . ." (Exod. 13:17-18). The Feast of Sukkos commemorates that meandering in the wilderness, for it was during those forty years that they received the Ten Commandments and the pattern of the Tabernacle.

The most important kinds of growth and development cannot be hurried. A nation of slaves needs more than ten days to become a nation of free men capable of governing themselves under God. The bitter lesson of history reminds us that even after a two-year period the nation of Israel had not learned to believe God enough to claim His promise. It took an additional thirty-eight years of wandering for the unbelievers to die in order that the younger generation might have the necessary faith to claim the promise.

When St. Chrysostom advised, "Depart from the highway and transplant thyself in some enclosed ground, for it is hard for a tree which stands by the wayside to keep her fruit till it be ripe," he called our attention to one of the highest purposes of higher educational institutions. "To keep till her fruit be ripe" is another way of saying that it takes a long time to bring excellence to maturity. Implicit in every worthy college program is the understanding that producing the fruit of an enlightened mind, a disciplined will and a sensitive, responsive heart is a time-consuming, costly process.

A parent once approached a college president and asked, "How long will it take you to educate my son?" "That all depends on what you want your son to become," replied the president. "It takes nature two weeks to grow a squash and a hundred years to grow an oak."

A person or society has not been Christianized unless the "law of the harvest" has been understood and accepted. The pleasure principle impatiently casts off that which deprives of immediate need-satisfaction, what postpones, what hints of waiting, earning, delaying. Show us a button to push, a handle to turn — whatever provides what we want *now*. When self discipline breaks down to the point where the present receives the total emphasis, there usually follows an accent on sensual pleasure. This short-cut philosophy was expressed by Aldous Huxley who said:

> As far as I can see the only possible new pleasure would be derived from the invention of a new drug which would provide a harmless substitute for alcohol. If we could sniff or swallow something that would abolish inferiority, atone us with our fellows in a glowing exultation of affection and make life in all its aspects seem not only worth living but divinely beautiful and significant, and if this heavenly world-transforming drug were of such a kind that we could wake up next morning with a clear head and undamaged constitution, then it seems to me that all our problems would be solved and earth would be a paradise.[8]

Those who see deeper into the realities of life believe Huxley's thinking to be a trumpet with an uncertain sound. A vastly clearèr note was struck by Dr. Charles

Malik, the former president of the United Nations, who said, "I am not foolish enough to believe that today or tomorrow the world is going to be radically changed. There is no shortcut to heaven except through the healing influence of Jesus Christ." Reported in *The Houston Post,* April 11, 1969.

You will find the background for a third suggestion in I Kings 7 in the description of the magnificent temple built by Solomon. Tucked away in that chapter is a verse that reads like this: "And upon the top of the pillars was lily work . . ." (vs. 22a). What was the reason for taking the time, expense and effort to decorate the top of the massive pillars? Ah! How insensitive would he be who could not sense an aura of the sacred that surrounds the answer to that question! It suggests the very meaning and purpose of worship. Carving lily work upon the top of the pillars is deeply symbolic of the fruit of a right relationship to God. For the man whose life is devoted to God's glory is motivated by what pleases the Object of his devotion.

When Michelangelo was putting the finishing touches on some figures in a remote area of the ceiling of the Sistine Chapel, one of his friends asked, "Why do you take such pains with what nobody will know about?"

"I will," replied the great artist.

Solomon and Michelangelo exemplify those whose efforts are expressions of the greatness and humility of love. This spirit resides in the words of One whom Solomon and Michelangelo would have wanted in their company: "Whatsoever ye do, do it heartily, as unto the Lord and not unto men" (Col. 3:23).

But there is more to this last point. Putting lily work upon the pillar tops carries with it not only the importance of deeds but dreams. It gets beneath the behavior to the motives. As time passes you will come to realize that no way of life enables one to satisfy every desire. Not all our dreams will be fulfilled in this life. We, too, like Browning's Rabbi ben Ezra should be able to say, "What I aspired to be, and was not, comforts me."

Actually Solomon's father, King David, wanted more than anything else to build the Temple. Even though David's final ambition was not realized, God said to him: "Whereas it was in thine heart to build an house unto my name, thou didst well that it was in thine heart" (I Kings 8:18). Your future will be divinely blessed if by your dreams and deeds you spend it carving lily work upon the pillar of your life. As someone has said, "Your life is God's gift to you; what you do with it is your gift to God."

Those whose philosophy of life embraces living in accordance with God's will, a willingness to develop in the wilderness and the desire to make life an effort to bring glory to the Creator will want to join with Dr. John Hunter who wrote:

> Dear Master, in whose Life I see
> All that I long and fail to be,
> Let Thy clear light for ever shine,
> To shame and guide this life of mine.

> Though what I dream and what I do
> In my poor days are always two,
> Help me, oppressed by things undone,
> O Thou, Whose dreams and deeds were one.

3

When You Land in Troas

Wise was he who said that every man's life is a diary in which he starts out to write one thing and is forced to write another. An adequate conception of life must embrace and integrate life's experiences that force the "diary" to read different from what was originally intended. Granted, few college graduates entertain such thoughts while moving the tassel. Later on, however, the sons and daughters of Alma Mater confront those unexpected and undesirable diary-changing experiences and find themselves needing the resources of a theologically conceived philosophy of life. These experiences are primarily those that cause suffering. They include failure, disappointment, deprivation and shock.

One such experience came to a man whose life had undergone profound change. Students of the New Testament will recall how Saul, the chief persecutor of the early Christians became Paul, the great leader of those whom he had persecuted. After encountering Christ on the road to Damascus, Paul, consumed by the passion to share his conversion experience, began to travel in the service of his new Master. As time passed he developed the desire to travel to Bithynia, the richest province of Asia. The day came when he set sail for the place to which he had dreamed of going, to spread the good news of the Gospel. Instead of arriving at his chosen destination, however, Paul found himself in lowly Troas, an unimportant city on the coast of Mysia.

This true account of Paul is the story of every man. We all have our Bithynias, for Bithynia is the symbol of fondest dream fulfillment, the place where our hopes are to be realized and great desires are to be satisfied. And so we set sail, only to land in Troas, the place of disappointment, heartache, frustration.

The ways in which we respond to a Troas experience probably explain better than anything else the difference between men. Admittedly we are affected by environment; yet, the final truth is that it is not what happens to us, but how we react to what happens to us that determines the course of our lives. The Psalmist said, "That man is blessed who, going through the vale of misery, uses it for a well" (Ps. 84:6).

When we land in Troas we are tempted to ask, Why me? This is usually asked in reference to individual merit and implies a belief that suffering is payment for unworthy living. Thus the conflict: on the one hand, we have a sense of worth; on the other we are experiencing what is only supposed to happen to the unworthy. It is precisely here that the Troas experience threatens to overwhelm us. For if it cannot be explained as punishment, it seems meaningless. Although Nietzsche was an atheist, he recognized the importance

34

of a philosophy of life when he said, "He who has a *why* to live for can bear almost any *how.*"

Twenty-eight-year-old Stephen Crane told of a man who said to the universe, "Sir, I exist!" And the universe replied, "However, the fact has not created in me a sense of obligation."

As Dr. Leslie Weatherhead has pointed out, all of us suffer through the human family's ignorance, folly and sin, as well as through our own. But he rightly believes that God desires to replace ignorance with knowledge, folly with wisdom, and sin with holiness. Therefore, he who clings to this belief will be spared the error of attributing whatever is the result of ignorance, folly or sin to the will of God.

Sometimes when we land in Troas we react the wrong way. We come to regret the impulsive act, the willful sin, the foolish words. In these times it is well to remember the lesson that Dr. Weatherhead learned when he was a young British officer in World War I. During an assignment to India he was given an opportunity to observe the great skills of the rug-weavers. As he passed among the workers, he turned to his guide and asked, "What happens if the weaver makes a mistake?" The guide answered, "If he is a great enough artist, he will weave the mistake into the pattern." We who are Christians have the assurance that the Divine Artist is great enough to take even our blunders and weave them into the pattern of a life that will glorify Him. As the Apostle Paul has said, "And we know that all things work together for good to them that love God, to them who are the called according to His purpose" (Rom. 8:28).

Although no one would *choose* the Troas experiences

of life, it is possible to *use* them in cooperation with God's higher purposes. For it was in unwanted Troas that Paul received the Macedonian call. Out of his disappointment in Troas, Paul received the vision that led to the spreading of the Christian message to Europe.

Troas teaches lessons that could never be learned in Bithynia. A psychoanalyst once had under his care a talented young playwright. This promising young patient was brilliant, possessing craftsmanship, keen dramatic sense and style, sharp powers of observation and general knowledge of the world. Yet he was a failure. Giving his reason for his patient's failure, Dr. Theodor Reik wrote: "He always chooses the easy way out of his conflicts; he will not stand his ground in the face of unavoidable grief, sorrow, despair."[1] In removing himself from stressful, unpleasant situations the would-be artist deprived himself of that knowledge which can only be purchased with personal suffering.

> No, when the fight begins within himself,
> A man's worth something. God stoops o'er his head,
> Satan looks up between his feet — both Tug —
> He's left himself in the middle: the soul wakes
> And grows. Prolong that battle through his life!
> — Robert Browning

Kahlil Gibran, in his book *The Wanderer,* tells the story of one oyster who spoke to a neighboring oyster, "I have a very great pain within me. It is heavy and round and I am in distress." Came the haughty, complacent reply, "Praise be to the heavens and to the sea, I have no pain within me. I am well and whole both within and without." A crab passing by overheard the conversation and said to the one who thought himself

36

totally well, "Yes, you are well and whole; but the pain that your neighbor bears is a pearl of exceeding beauty."[2] Dr. Gordon Allport, the great psychologist of Harvard, has said, "Mental health requires that we learn to grow muscles where our injuries were."

New dimensions to understanding, compassion, sensitivity, and the entire life style are added by the proper reactions to the Troas experience.

> I walked a mile with Pleasure;
> She chattered all the way,
> But left me none the wiser
> For all she had to say.
>
> I walked a mile with Sorrow
> And ne'er a word said she;
> But oh, the things I learned from her
> When sorrow walked with me!
> — Robert Browning Hamilton
> *Along the Road*

One who unhesitantly endorses this truth is none other than America's new first citizen. After suffering the loss of the Presidential election in 1960 and just two years later failing in an effort to be elected governor of his home state of California, Richard Nixon's political career seemed at an end. His remarkable comeback was climaxed in 1968 when the nation elected him its 37th President. Reflecting on his Troas experiences President Nixon stated, "There is too much emphasis on winning. There's a lot to be learned from losing, too. Both success and adversity teach, but adversity teaches more."[3]

The wisest man of the world of his day gave this counsel: "It is better to go to the house of mourning, than to go to the house of feasting. . . . Sorrow is better than laughter: for by the sadness of the countenance the heart is made wiser" (Eccles. 7:2, 3).

A young pastor sat beside the hospital bed in which his wife lay. It was nearing the time for them to become parents. During the long night hours he read *Invitation to Pilgrimage* by John Baillie. Soon they were to bask together in the glow of the proud father's announcement: "It's a boy." Later they were to begin a desperate search for some specialist who could help the little lad, but they were unsuccessful — little Ronnie was mentally handicapped.

The entrance of this father into the school of suffering taught him many things. Recalling that first grief-fraught summer, Dr. Ronald Meredith wrote, "Grief teaches lessons that joy can never know. We discovered that there is a comradeship in pain."

Dr. Meredith now looks forward to that great day when God's plan for us will be perfected. He believes that one day he will look at Ronnie and say, "Hi, Son," and for the first time he will respond intelligently, smile and say, "Hi, Dad." They will need a lot of time to talk, for Ronnie has never been able to speak a word.[4]

So we learn to prefer Troas with its vision instead of Bithynia without it. This preference does not come cheaply learned. Our faith will be tested; at times we will agonize with doubts, loneliness and a deep sense of futility. During these times keep your heart unhardened and turned toward Him "who is not an high priest who cannot be touched by the feeling of our infirmities." Then you will gain the insight of the unknown writer who penned these tender and penetrating lines:

VALLEY OF SORROW

I came to the valley of sorrow
    And dreary it looked to my view,
But Jesus was walking beside me,
    And sweetly we journeyed through.

And now I look to that valley
    As the fairest that ever I trod,
For I learned there the love of my Father,
    I leaned on the arm of my God.

And if some day the Father should ask me
    Which was the best path I trod.
How quickly my heart shall make answer,
    "The valley of sorrow, O God!"
                    — Anonymous

Life takes on deeper meaning because of its Troas experiences. Without suffering there would be no great music, literature or art. Many agree with Alan Paton, the great South African Christian who believes "that the alternative to a universe in which there is no suffering, in which evil struggles with good and cruelty with mercy, would be a universe of nothingness, where there would be neither good nor evil, no happiness, only an eternity of uninterrupted banality."[5]

It is well to go on to observe that Troas is *not* a permanent state. Paul moved on to Europe. The Christian's hope is based on the knowledge that no valley is endless; no burden will remain unlifted. If time has to stretch into eternity the deepest yearnings of the human heart will have fulfillment. "Eye hath not seen, nor ear heard, neither have entered into the heart of man the things which God hath prepared for them that love him" (I Cor. 2:9).

In facing the Troas experiences of life we cannot attempt to explain the mystery of suffering. This is the theme of Job, the oldest book of the Bible. Job knew the pain of personal sickness, the grief over loss of family, the dismay over distorted counsel of friends. But these calamities failed to defeat him. In fact the great Old Testament sufferer could say: ". . . Thou shalt forget thy misery, and remember it as waters that pass away" (Job. 11:16).

Christians look forward with John to the new heaven and new earth when "God shall wipe away all tears from their eyes; and there shall be no more death, neither sorrow, nor crying, neither shall there be any more pain" (Rev. 21:4).

The Secret Hidden from the Wise

There is something peculiarly winsome about the undergraduate who, when asked by Dean DeVane of Yale, "Are you in the upper half of your class?" replied, "No, sir, I'm in the half that makes the upper half possible."

Whether they are in the top half or the bottom half of their class, what is it that graduates are most concerned with? Obviously there are many authoritative replies that could be given to this question. A growing number of qualified observers, however, would agree that this concern was expressed by one of Camus' characters in the play *Caligula*:

> To lose one's life is a little thing, and I will have the courage when necessary. But to see the sense of this life dissipated, to see our reason for existence disappear, this is what is intolerable. A man cannot live without meaning.

More than a hint of the answer to this problem is what you are wearing on your finger and the sheepskin you received at commencement. Senior rings and degrees are not worth much in themselves. *It is that which they symbolize that makes them so meaningful.*

John Steinbeck has Joe Saul express this idea in his *Burning Bright.* Upon hearing from his wife that they were expecting a child, Saul, ecstatic with joy, confided to a close friend: "I want to bring a present to her . . . something like a ceremony, something like a golden sacrament, some pearl like a prayer or a red flaming ruby of thanks . . . I must get this thing. My joy requires a symbol."

We realize that a symbol gets its enormous power from the actuality which it suggests. Carlyle explained it in terms of the combination of speech plus silence. It is the silence — the ethereal world of the infinite — giving opportunity to the imagination that sounds the depths of reality. Deriving meaning from life then is intimately linked with the ability to comprehend symbol.

The sad truth is that the subject of the following poem represents masses of modern men:

> O why do you walk through the fields in gloves,
>   Missing so much and so much?
> O fat white lady whom nobody loves,
> Why do you walk through the fields in gloves,
> When the grass is soft as the breast of doves
>   And shivering sweet to the touch?
> O why do you walk through the fields in gloves,
>   Missing so much and so much?
>
>   — Frances Cornford

That is our problem. Meaninglessness is the result of "wearing gloves," being out of contact with life in its most thrilling expressions. How then do we take the "gloves" off? By seeing the ideal through the real attempts to discover meaning are efforts to comprehend the ideal through the real, the essence through the form. This is why the poet may make a greater contribution to man than the scientist. By this is not meant mere rhyme-making for the metric cadence of some written form. Poethood in essence consists of entering into mystery, of seeing into the nature of things, of celebrating the commonplace. The poet is endowed with this gift of penetration. Because he sees through the material to the spiritual, the poet becomes everyman's interpreter of ultimate knowledge. He listens to the noise of the world's tragedies and hears the harmony of eternal purposes. He looks at the fragments of man's experiences and sees the integrating essence which results in a grasp of wholeness.

Life can become dull prose unless we bring to it the poet's gift. Perhaps we cannot be scientific in our study of life, but the history of man's experience reveals a need about which psychology textbooks are strangely silent. In the last few years a system of thought called logo-therapy has found growing acceptance. Viktor Frankl, the Viennese psychotherapist who fathered it, believes that man's deepest need is to find meaning for his life. Without satisfaction of this need we suffer the most serious deprivations; we walk with weights on our heels; we endure the human condition of being mastered by the mundane. What we need is wings for the spirit. We must find majesty, nobility and high purpose in living.

Elizabeth Barrett Browning's poem, "Aurora Leigh," takes up the theme of the progress of mankind. Here is the way the poetess expressed herself:

> . . . It takes a soul
> To move a body: it takes a high-souled man,
> To move the masses, even to a cleaner style:
> It takes the ideal, to blow a hair's-breadth off
> The dust of the actual. . . .

It would not be difficult to so lose oneself in the beauty of these lines and miss their message. Life has a way of remaining unchanged. Harsh realities seem to be fixed, defying man's best efforts to improve his world. But there is the deeper problem, that of the "actual" without the "ideal."

Is this not a matter of "seeing through?" And is this not the reason why art, music and literature are an integral part of most college curriculums? Since art is the expression of the ideal through the real, most art forms are symbols, expressing the hidden to those with eyes to see.

We see only what we are inwardly prepared to see. We see things not as they are, but as we are, for each of us brings to experience a unique history of development. All that characterizes our reactions to and affirmations of life — education, models, influences — are opticians of the soul, determining our perceptions of events, experiences and ideas. Meanings, therefore, become private property of the individual. What happens on the human level when relationships are impoverished and deprived of the joys of spontaneous sharing because of a deficient response by a "glove-wearer" is contained in the following dialogue:

> The stars are out tonight.
> Oh? said the other.
> The moon hangs suspended in the sky.
> Oh? said the other.

44

Take my hand and let's enter it all.
O.K. said the other.
And the solitary entrance was made.

The most adequate response to reality is exemplified by the central figure of the four Gospels. A careful reading of the Gospels of Matthew, Mark, Luke and John reveals the clearest eyes that ever focused on this little planet. To Jesus the whole world was a symbol. Everything He saw on earth reminded Him of something He knew about heaven. These insights He shared with others in parables, which have been defined as "earthly stories of heavenly truths." He knew that creation is the art of God. In poet-like fashion, Christ "saw through" the expressed to the Expresser and taught men of His love and plan of redemption: "For God so loved the world that he gave his only begotten Son that whosoever believeth in him should not perish, but have everlasting life" (John 3:16).

If every man yearns for meaning for his life, and if "meaning" consists in "blowing the dust off the actual" and getting to the "ideal," then how do we develop the ability to "see"? The answer lies in Christ's reply to the disciples' question, "Why speakest thou . . . in parables?" "Unto you," He answered, "it is given to know the mysteries of the kingdom of heaven, but to them it is not given. For whosoever hath, to him shall be given, and he shall have more abundance; but whosoever hath not, from him shall be taken away even that he hath. Therefore speak I to them in parables: because they seeing see not, and hearing they hear not, neither do they understand" (Matt. 13:10-13). Why?

"For this people's heart is waxed gross. . . ." There

45

we have it. The eye of understanding gets its focus from the heart: "Blessed are the pure in heart, for they shall see God." Comprehending heavenly mystery is not simply a matter of the intellect. What determines our ability to perceive God's expressions of Himself (life's deepest meaning) is the changed heart rather than the educated head. Thus the parable became Christ's way to manifest the way of life under God so that men would be lured by the manifestation and be led through inquiry and obedience to the concealed, supreme reality of the eternal. This is the meaning of Albert Schweitzer's statement:

> His words are the same, "Follow thou me!" and he puts us to the tasks which he has to carry out in our age. He commands. He will reveal himself through all that they are privileged to experience in His fellowship of peace and activity, of struggle and suffering, till they come to know, as an inexpressible secret, Who He is.

One of the most fascinating encounters in all of literature is recorded in the seventh chapter of the Book of Mark. Study carefully the dialogue that is contained in the encounter, for it illustrates an unforgettable experience in "seeing through":

> And from thence he arose, and went into the borders of Tyre and Sidon, and entered into an house, and would have no man know it: but he could not be hid.
> For a certain woman, whose young daughter had an unclean spirit, heard of him, and came and fell at his feet:
> The woman was a Greek, a Syrophenician by nation; and she besought him that he would cast forth the devil out of her daughter.
> But Jesus said unto her, Let the children first be

46

filled: for it is not meet to take the children's bread, and to cast it unto the dogs.

And she answered and said unto him, Yes, Lord: yet the dogs under the table eat of the children's crumbs.

And he said unto her, For this saying go thy way; the devil is gone out of thy daughter.

And when she was come to her house, she found the devil gone out, and her daughter laid upon the bed.

If we interpret Christ's responses — His initial silence, His first remarks — as insensitivity and harshness, we are probably too literal minded. The woman was not so limited. She "saw through" the words (the actual) to Christ Himself. Missing from the recorded dialogue are those vitally important non-verbal aspects — facial expression, voice tone, gestures of hands, eye movements — that convey meanings beyond the power of words. Instead of thinking that Christ was being intentionally rude, the sharp-witted Canaanite recognized the bantering nature of what he said. Her reply expresses her understanding of what He *really* meant and thus reflected her recognition of who He really *was*.

This Syrophenician woman exhibited the kind of skill with symbols (words) that would rank her high in any graduating class. A most reliable way to predict scholastic success is to test for word mastery as evidenced by vocabulary tests and writing exercises. The claim that scholastic aptitude is revealed by command of language finds statistical support. Those who show the greatest facility with words have often shown the greatest power to understand. A command over the symbolic power of language is usually indicative of a capacity to learn relations and group concepts, to perceive the deeper reality, to comprehend essence.

"In the beginning was the Word, and the Word was with God, and the Word was God. The Word was made flesh and dwelt among us" (John 1:1).

Knowledge of the prime reality is gained by man through the Word. By accepting the Word, man relates himself to the Eternal. This relationship effects such a revolutionary change that it could be said by one who had experienced this change that, "If any man be in Christ he is a new creature: behold old things are passed away; behold all things are become new" (II Cor. 5:17).

Language forms the symbolic bridge to spiritual reality. "Seeing through" by means of language leads to the concept of community. In the breakdown of relationships among men in our world, a new effort must be made to show what holds people together, relates them to one another, and nourishes these relationships. Is this possible if truth exists and is attainable by man? If so, this would mean differences in attainment, in ability to "see through." Those who do not recognize degrees of differences in attainment show themselves deniers of such a reality. Lacking an objective basis for their appeals, they decry the division that inevitably results when values hold sway. Human relationships deteriorate when men lack the collective ability to comprehend those ideals which have socially integrating power. Christ was perfectly aware of the effects of His coming to earth. He said, "Suppose ye that I am come to give peace on earth? I tell you nay but rather . . . a sword." Is violence then the inevitable alternative? Will might furnish the standard for the right? Divisions

48

among men demand charity, which is the Christian cohesive. We know that unbelievers cannot grant Christ's basis of distinction; but then they must be called upon to provide a better ground for charity which, as all thinking people realize, holds the key.

In welcoming a class of freshmen to his college a devout Christian president recalled when he was a fourteen-year-old boy on a camping trip to the Carter County Caves in Kentucky. He and some of his companions found themselves far back in the darkness of one of the caves. Crawling along on a ledge with their guide, they saw by the light of their lanterns the geological wonders of the stalactites and stalagmites upon the wall of a nearby cave. Then, as they turned a corner, a wall covered with the engravings made by other groups of campers on earlier days came into view. To his great delight the college mentor discovered his own father's initials scrawled on the wall many years before. That deeply moving experience later became symbolic. Many college students would hear him say that college could give them a light and put a lantern in their hand. But their journey in the sometimes dark cave of life would never be complete unless at some momentous turn they discovered the Father's name.

This discovery provides the richest meaning of life. It was the discovery of the Canaanite. Beneath the witty verbal exchange in her encounter with Christ there lay the true secret of how to exalt the commonplace and ennoble the ordinary. It is this secret that is hidden from the worldly wise. For the secret is the ability to see through that which is revealed, to that which is unrevealed. But what is the ability to "see through," to get the point, if it is not another name for a *sense of humor?* And if it is purity of heart that clears the eyes of the understanding, do we not come to a most astonishing conclusion — that in the truest, most profound sense, it takes a saint to have a sense of humor!

5

"I Prayed... for Help and Guidance"

Most of us graduate with a degree — of difficulty. This was especially true of one fellow who after much struggle had completed the requirements for graduation at a certain university. While he was joyfully awaiting the final ceremony and his diploma, he received this note from an aunt: "Please let me know the date of your graduation, so I can send a token of my astonishment!"

A story is told of an eager young surveyor just graduated from college. His first assignment was to inspect a section of highway that was frequently flooded. He was told to choose a good site and to erect a warning sign for traffic. He chose a site close to the lowest part of the road. There he put up a sign which read:

"Notice is hereby given that when this sign is under water the road is impassable."

A second thought, however, leads to the realization that college graduates have had at least four years of

51

post high school experience in learning what happens to "the best laid plans of mice and men."

Studies show for example that most freshmen who decide on a major change their minds by the junior year. In addition it has been estimated that as high as 40 per cent of all graduate students choose a graduate field of study different from their undergraduate major. As we become more aware of the importance of wise planning, we are also developing an increasing appreciation for the complications involved. A couple were married while still in college. Little did they anticipate the difficulties they would encounter during their last year of school. Recalling them, the young wife sighed, "That was the year that we got an M.A., a B.A. and a B.A.B.Y."

Our rapidly changing world adds to our ineptness in meeting life's crises, making planning difficult. Technological changes are now so swift that skills and training quickly become obsolete. A certain patient who could not sleep was advised by the doctor to have a bite to eat before he went to bed. "But doctor," protested the patient, "two months ago you told me never to eat anything before going to bed."

"I know," said the doctor, "but science has made enormous strides since then."

In the face of all this how can one plan wisely for the future? First, a discovery of where the rocks are must be made. This is illustrated by the experience of three fishermen who were anchored about a hundred yards off shore. The fishing was poor and one of the anglers decided to go ashore. He stepped over the side and walked across the water to the beach. No sooner had his feet touched the sand when another of the men announced that he too was going ashore. As the third man looked on with astonishment, his buddy duplicated the performance of the first man.

"Well," thought the man who remained in the boat, "if they can do it, so can I." And over the side he went, plunging straight to the bottom. He came sputtering and splashing back to the surface and climbed back into the boat. Not one to give up too quickly, he tried several more times but with the same unhappy results.

During this time the man's two fishing partners had been watching this side-splitting demonstration. Finally one of them managed to stop laughing long enough to say to the other, "He'll drown himself if we don't hurry and tell him where the rocks are!"

Unless one knows where the "rocks" are, the journey is hazardous indeed. For us the rocks symbolize the principles of a meaningful, productive, richly satisfying way of life. Where are the rocks? They lie beneath the waves of an uncertain future, but they are there.

When the late Dr. William Lyon Phelps taught his popular literature courses at Yale he used to say, "I would rather have a knowledge of the Bible without a college education than a college education without a knowledge of the Bible." This great scholar had discovered the Book that tells where the rocks are. "Thy word," said King David, "is a lamp unto my feet and a light unto my pathway."

It is advantageous to have directions for the journey, but to have a Guide is even better. The Creator of the map is best qualified to give reliable instructions and willingly offers not only His counsel but His companionship: "I will instruct thee and teach thee in the way which thou shalt go . . ." (Ps. 32:8).

The greatest sermon ever taught was ended by the following words which ring with Divine authority:

> Therefore whosoever heareth these sayings of mine, and doeth them, I will liken him unto a wise man, which built his house upon a rock:
> And the rain descended, and the floods came, and the winds blew, and beat upon that house; and it fell not: for it was founded upon a rock.
> And everyone that heareth these sayings of mine, and doeth them not, shall be likened unto a foolish man, which built his house upon the sand:
> And the rain descended, and the floods came, and the winds blew, and beat upon that house; and it fell: and great was the fall of it.
> And it came to pass, when Jesus had ended these sayings, the people were astonished at his doctrine:
> For he taught them as one having authority, and not as the scribes.
>
> — Matt. 7:24-29

So certain is Jesus Christ about the results of living life His way that He said, "My doctrine is not mine, but his that sent me. If any man will do his will, he shall know of the doctrine, whether it be of God, or whether I speak of myself" (John 7:16b, 17). If those who question the authority of Christ's words will obey them, they will come to know experientially that there is a way of life that reveals by its unfolding nature the fact of Providential care and guidance.

As an adventurous youth, Winston Churchill was captured in November, 1899, while serving as a correspondent in the Boer War. He was taken to the Pretoria prison camp in the interior of South Africa. On the night of December 12, 1899, he escaped along with two British officers who shortly gave up. His own situation looked hopeless. He was 300 miles from the frontier, could not speak a word of the Boer language (Afrikaans, a local form of Dutch) and had neither a map nor a compass. He carried 75 British pounds and four slabs of chocolate in his pocket. Nevertheless, he began following the railroad and finally managed to climb into a freight car. Before daylight could reveal his presence, young Churchill leaped off the train and spent the day in hiding. Gradually he became possessed of a sense of desperation and horror. Hungry, exhausted and dismayed, he was forced to face the grim truth: "No exercise of my own feeble wit and strength could save me from my enemies . . . I prayed long and earnestly for help and guidance."

At last Churchill spotted some white men's houses. Were the occupants friendly? Too exhausted to really care, he knocked at the front door. He was invited in by an Afrikaans-speaking man holding a gun in his hand. As the future prime minister revealed his identity, his capture and escape, the man listened in silence. Then he slowly walked over and locked the door. The almost unbearable suspense came to an end when the man turned and walked toward Churchill, holding out his hand. "Thank God you have come here," he said, "it is the only house for twenty miles where you would not have been handed over." Assured that he was with fellow Britishers, Churchill recalls, "I felt like a drowning man pulled out of the water and informed he has won the derby." His prayer for direction had been answered.

This great possibility of being providentially led was also William Cullen Bryant's conviction when he wrote

"To A Water Fowl":

> He who, from zone to zone,
> Guides through the boundless sky thy certain flight,
> In the long way that I must tread alone
> Will lead my steps aright.

The second principle of successful planning is that of preparing for life's inevitable experiences.

Billy Graham told a group of students at the University of California about a college girl who was fatally injured in a car accident. As her life ebbed away, she spoke these last words to her mother: "Mother, you taught me everything I needed to know to get by in college. You taught me how to light my cigarette, how to hold my cocktail glass, and how to have intercourse safely. But Mother, you never taught me how to die. You better teach me quickly, Mother, because I'm dying."

Long ago there lived a brilliant teacher named Saint Philip Neri, whose knowledge of the law had gained him a far-reaching reputation. Eager young students would travel great distances to sit at the feet of this learned scholar. Each new student was given an entrance exam that can be described as follows:

> "Why did you come?" he would begin.
> "To study law," was the standard reply.
> "What will you do upon completion of your studies?"
> "I will set up my practice."
> "And after that?"
> "I will get married and have a family."
> "What then?"
> "I will enjoy my home and my work."
> "Then what?"
> "Then I will grow older and eventually die."
> "And after death, what then?"

56

In this manner the great teacher would guide the student to the most certain of life's experiences — ". . . it is appointed unto men once to die, but after this the judgment" (Heb. 9:27). Saint Philip understood that the student could not truly be ready to live unless he was ready to die. Alexander Dumas expressed it like this: "If the end be well, all is well."

Wise planning also emphasizes adequate preparation for those "common ventures" of life, such as marriage, parenthood, and work. Successful living can be explained in terms of how well we succeed in these major areas of our lives.

A third principle of successful planning may be seen in the words of the following poem:

> I plan for the future.
> I yearn for the past.
> And, meantime, the present
> Is leaving me fast.
> — Anonymous

Dr. William Osler, the world famous physician, writer and lecturer, tells of the time when he was a young medical student facing his final examinations. Worry as to the future was giving him much distress. Like so many others who travel the path to the degree, he was uncertain about the next stage of his life. Although he had survived the difficult academic journey, he bore the telltale description of the student, being "lean and pale and leaden-eyed with study." While under the burden of so many question marks, young Osler picked up a volume of Carlyle. On the first page he read a sentence which he credits with changing his life. The famous sentence? "Our main business is not to see what lies dimly at a distance, but to do what lies clearly at hand."

Some forty-two years later, by then respected around the world, Dr. Osler accepted an invitation to deliver the Silliman lectures at Yale University. On the evening of Sunday, April 20, 1913, Dr. Osler delivered to the Yale students an address that has become a literary classic. Entitled "A Way of Life," the address underscores the futility of needless concern for what has happened in the past and an overconcern for what may happen in the future. "The day of man's salvation is NOW — the life of the present, of today, lived earnestly, intently, without a forward-looking thought, is the only insurance for the future."

In the very same college, some twenty-eight years before Dr. Osler's historic address, a sophomore named William Lyon Phelps was wondering about what he was going to do with his life. After a great deal of fruitless worry he took his problem to an older man who gave this wise advice: "You have nearly three years before you graduate; you should not give the matter a thought; you cannot make any decision until the emergency comes; haven't you got a lesson for tomorrow? Sit down and study it. Live one day at a time."

Phelps thought the advice was sound and tried to follow it. Nevertheless, as the semester swiftly passed, he found himself, with commencement only a few weeks away, still without knowledge of what profession to follow. His interests had flowered in three fields — the ministry, journalism, and teaching. "As it turned out, however," wrote Dr. Phelps, looking back over his brilliant, productive life, "my life has been spe the practice of all three professions; and indeed at this moment, I am a teacher, a preacher, and a journalist."

What will the '70's hold for you? Graduate school? The draft? Marriage? Parenthood? Getting started in your life's work? As you ponder your future remember the words of wise King Solomon:

> Trust in the Lord with all thine heart;
> and lean not unto thine own understanding.
> In all thy ways acknowledge him
> and he shall direct thy paths.
>
> — Prov. 3:5, 6

The path He charts for you is "out there." It leads to the deepest personal satisfaction, social enrichment and spiritual fulfillment. In this connection the following words are deeply meaningful:

> And I said to the man who stood at the gate of the year: "Give me a light that I may tread safely into the unknown." And he replied: "Go out into the darkness and put your hand into the hand of God. That shall be to you better than a light and safer than a known way." So I went forth and, finding the hand of God, trod gladly into the night. And He led me toward the hills and the breaking of dawn in the lone East.

Graduation time brings to you a colon stage of your life. You do not know what the days ahead will bring. But you can stride confidently into your future if your life belongs to the One to whom your future belongs. His help will be given you as it was to a young leader of long ago who, like you, was at the colon stage of his life. He was assured that divine guidance is given "that ye may know the way by which ye must go: for ye have not passed this way before" (Joshua 3:4b). Your future success is certain if you can say with the poetess:

> I do not ask thy way to understand,
>   My way to see;
> Better in darkness just to grasp thy hand
>   And follow thee.
>   — Minnie Louise Haskins
>   in *God Knows*

6

A Faith for Times Like These

Recently a number of prominent Americans were asked to give their views on the condition of the American spirit today. The following are some excerpts taken from their thought-provoking responses:

> The sickness of American society . . . does not reside in the existence of problems. Nor does it reside in the existence of discontent, ferment and rebelliousness. This traditionally has been the health of our society. Our sickness resides rather in our incapacity to deal effectively with our problems — an incapacity which has begun to suffuse our nation with an ominous sense of impotence.[1] — Arthur Schlesinger, Jr., historian

> The age of the "mass man" has arrived. Man now is frightened, anxious, lonely. He cannot understand the changes, he does not know their causes, he has no idea where they will lead him, he has not yet gained a new frame of orientation and devotion which would fit his changing world.[2] — Erich Fromm, psychoanalyst

> With a few notable exceptions, the intellectual has helped to compound our spiritual chaos. We are told

61

by many voices that standards no longer apply, that there is no good or evil, right or wrong; that the function of the artist is to express himself rather than communicate with others, that it is enough for him to reflect the violence and anarchy in our life without providing a vision of a better one.[3] — Marya Marnes, social critic

I believe that the condition of the American spirit is due to our adherence to several illusions . . . that money and things bring happiness and peace of mind . . . that peace is a cause rather than an effect . . . that man is naturally good . . . that religion without personal commitment and involvement is enough. . . . The great question is: How can we rediscover the faith which was once a dynamic revolutionary, life-changing force in our society.[4] — Billy Graham, evangelist

Others who respond to the younger generation's request to "tell it like it is" would point out the following conditions facing your graduating class:

1. *Environmental crises.* A recent conference was called by the U.S. National Commission for UNESCO. The conference, entitled "Man and His Environment . . . A View Toward Survival" had 75 speakers and 450 delegates. The most generally agreed upon problem was the population explosion. Lee A. Dubridge, the science advisor to President Nixon said, "The first great challenge of our time is ensuring that there are no more births than deaths." Paul R. Erlich, a Stanford University biologist stated that the battle to feed humanity has already been lost. Several speakers warned that pollution of air and water could make a prophet of T. S. Eliot, who wrote:

> This is the way the world ends
> This is the way the world ends

> This is the way the world ends
> Not with a bang but a whimper.

One of the predictions made at this meeting was that the environmental crises will replace Viet Nam as the dominant issue in America on college campuses during the 1970's.

Ecologists tell us that the earth's population doubled in the last ninety years ending in 1950, when it reached an estimated 2.5 billion. Predictions are that it will double again in less than half that time.

While the world's population is growing at the rate of 2 per cent per year, the world's food supplies are growing at the rate of only 1 per cent per year. We used to hear this familiar sentence: "Half of all the world's children will go to bed hungry tonight." Now it goes like this: "Seventy per cent of the world's children will go to sleep hungry tonight."

2. *The dehumanizing effects of increased mechanization of life.* Automation has become an established part of our way of life. Some fear that man-versus-machine contests are becoming more and more a one-sided affair. Witness the set of computers that are supplementing the fatherly role of advising Sammy where to go to college. The memory cores of these computers are filled with facts and figures on almost three thousand U.S. colleges. Aided by their guidance counselors, students fill out questionnaires, giving their ability to pay, their preferences and their motives. This information is fed to the computer. Out comes a complete roster of possible colleges!

Computerization and automation are here to stay, but not without their effect on man. Morris Bishop, a

professor at Cornell University, expressed the deperson-
alizing effects of our times in the following:

> The fellows up in Personnel,
>> They have a set of cards on me.
> The sprinkled perforations tell
>> My individuality.
>
> And what am I? I am a chart
>> Upon the cards of IBM;
> The secret places of the heart
>> Have little secrecy for them.
>
> It matters not how I may prate,
>> They punch with punishments my scroll.
> The files are masters of my fate,
>> They are the captains of my soul.
>
> Monday my brain began to buzz;
>> I was in agony all night
> I found out what the trouble was:
>> They had my paper clip too tight.

Yet, a refreshing bit of news came from the University of Maryland recently. It seems that a computer
flunked arithmetic! Academic vice-president Hornbake
explained that the failure was due to an error in pro-
gramming. This caused the computer to issue incorrect
grade averages for several hundred students!

3. *Racial strife.* The social, economic, and psycho-
logical relationships between races are changing. The
colored peoples of the world constitute about three-
fourths of the world's population. The time has passed
when a man's skin color carries built-in advantages and
disadvantages. Performance, not pedigree, is what matters now. Privatism and prejudice must be replaced by
a general, societal growth toward brotherhood. Yours

is the generation that can achieve "liberty and justice for all."

4. *Lawlessness.* President Johnson's Special Commission on Law Enforcement and Administration of Justice reported the following startling statistics. Crime rates are rising more than six times as fast as our population. The 15-to-21-year-old age group had the highest arrest rate in the country. One boy in every six in the U.S. is referred to juvenile court. One-third of a sample of all Americans say it is unsafe to walk alone at night in their neighborhoods.

Much of our present lawlessness is caused by the more than 60,000 known hard-drug addicts, most of whom are between the ages of 21 and 30. The typical drug addict resorts to all kinds of crime to get money with which to buy the drugs he craves. This drains approximately $328 million a year from our economy.

5. *Failure to achieve lasting peace.* History has recorded the grim failure of man to achieve lasting peace. Starting with the Flood men have fought nearly 15,000 major and minor wars. Someone has estimated that one hundred million persons have perished in the wars and political persecutions of the 20th century alone.

When the late General Douglas MacArthur made his historic address in 1951 before the assembled Congress of the United States, he said that unless man could reverse the trend of world events "Armageddon will be at our door." The General continued, "The problem basically is theological and involves a spirit of recrudescence and improvement of human character . . . It must be of the spirit if we are to save the flesh."

Consider these more recent words by U-Thant: "I do not wish to seem overdramatic, but I can only conclude from the information that is available to me as Secretary-General that the members of the United Nations have perhaps ten years left in which to subordinate their ancient quarrels and launch a global partnership to curb the arms race, to improve the human environment, to defuse the population explosion, and to supply the required momentum to world development efforts.

"If such a global partnership is not formed within the next decade," he continued somberly before an assembly of bankers, diplomats, and professors, "then I very much fear that the problems I have mentioned will have reached such staggering proportions that they will be beyond our capacity to control."

All this makes the picture anything but appealing. It reminds one of the London policeman who, while walking his beat on the Waterloo bridge, spied a man about to jump. The bobby (London police are called bobbies) managed to get him just in time.

"Come now," said the bobby. "Tell me what is the matter. Is it money?"

The man shook his head.

"Is it your wife?"

Again a negative reply.

"Well, what is it then?" persisted the bobby.

"I'm worried about the condition of the world," admitted the man.

"Oh, come now," replied the bobby, reassuringly. "It couldn't be as bad as all that. Walk up and down the bridge with me and let's talk it over."

And so the two men walked along discussing the world's problems for about an hour and then they both jumped over!

6. *The secularization of society.* That Americans believe religion is losing its grip on our way of life is statistically demonstrable. Five Gallup surveys of Americans were made over an eleven year period from 1957 to 1968. The pollsters asked the same question in all surveys: "At the present time, do you think religion as a whole is increasing its influence on American life, or losing its influence?" The percentage of persons interviewed who believed that religion was losing influence rose from 14 percent in 1958 to 67 percent in 1968. According to Gallup those holding that view gave one of four reasons: (1) Young people are losing interest in formal religion — other influences are becoming more meaningful; (2) Growing crime, immorality and violence; (3) Materialistic distractions; and (4) The church is not playing its proper role — some accuse the church of not keeping up with the times, but as many say it is too involved in social and political issues.

Spiritual decay among college students may be reflected in the liberalization of their views toward heterosexual relationships. A recent Gallup survey of college students' attitudes toward sex showed that two out of every three interviewed think it is not wrong for men and women to have pre-marital sex relations. Their view was held by 72 per cent of the college males and 55 per cent of the coeds. Important attitudinal differences however were revealed on the basis of type of college attended. A majority of students who approved of pre-marital sex attended both public and private colleges. But the interviewers found that a majority of students attending church-related colleges held the opposite view.[5]

There are those who support the contention that the

67

wave of unrest sweeping over young people today is being generated by religious fervor and intense search for something in which to believe. Dr. John Siber, the Arts and Sciences Dean of the University of Texas observed: "Born during or soon after a global war with its atmosphere of violence, fear, tension, rush, loose morals, corruption and emphasis on materialism, the teen-agers and youngsters in their early 20's have learned the truth about Santa Claus." Dean Siber pointed out that today's students reject the authority of tradition. They want reasons and examples. What they object to are not the traditional standards, necessarily, but their elders' inconsistent attempts to live up to these standards. "They have discovered Santa Claus in all aspects of life," Siber said.

Today's college students have many questions to ask about the Christian faith. The two most frequently cited questions have to do with the uniqueness of Jesus Christ and the existence of a personal God. How can Christianity claim to be the one exclusive faith for all men? Is there a God who actually cares for the individual in a vast universe of impersonal law and force? This question was asked in another way by a certain coed who approached her professor of religion and said, "What I really want to know is this: Does God know my name?"

Galileo was accused of moving God too far out of the universe so that man began to feel discouraged and forsaken. His reply should have served to put the matter back into proper perspective in his day, but it should also have contemporary significance. "The sun," he said, "which has all those planets revolving about it and dependent on it for their orderly functions can ripen a bunch of grapes as if it had nothing else to do."

Pascal, the brilliant French scientist and mathematician of the seventeenth century, felt much the same as thoughtful members of your own generation. His inner quest for spiritual reality was given these words: "This is what I see that troubles me. I look on all sides and I find everywhere nothing but obscurity. Nature offers nothing which is not a subject of doubts and disquietude; if I saw nowhere any sign of a deity I should decide in the negative; if I saw everywhere the signs of a creator, I should rest in peace in my faith; but seeing too much to deny and too little confidently to affirm, I am in a pitiable state." Continuing to seek the answer, Pascal later came to realize, "I would not even seek Thee, hadn't Thou already found me."

What these times call for is a faith that anchors and sustains, that enables us to cope with change, stress, the unexpected, and to realize the divine expectation for our lives.

One night a distinguished ambassador lay sleepless in his bed. Worry over the future of his nation and of the world made him restless and anxious. Across the room lay his associate who finally turned to him and said, "May I ask you a question?"

"Of course," replied the ambassador.

"Sir," said the associate, "Do you believe that God governed the world before you and I came into it?"

"Indeed I do."

"Sir," continued the associate, "do you believe that God will govern the world after you and I are gone?"

"Of course."

"Sir," he said at last, "why can't you trust God to

govern the world while you and I are in it?" And with this irrefutable logic to calm him, the ambassador turned over and fell fast asleep.

The kind of faith we need in these turbulent times must help us overcome our weaknesses, strengthen our bonds with our fellowman and give mental stability. And this is exactly what Christ gives when we put our faith in Him. One who could write from direct experience stated: "For God hath not given us the spirit of fear; but of power, and of love, and of a sound mind" (II Tim. 1:7).

CREDO

Not what, but whom do I believe!
    That in my darkest hour of need,
    Hath comfort that no mortal creed
    To mortal man may give.
Not what, but whom!
    For Christ is more than all the creeds
    And His full life of gentle deeds
    Shall all the creeds outlive.
Not what, but whom!
    Who walks beside me in the gloom?
    Who shares the burden wearisome?
    Who all the dim way doth illume?
    And bids me look beyond the tomb
    The larger life to live?
Not what I do believe, but whom!
    Not what, but whom!

— John Oxenham

7

The Fifth Year and the Green Altar

One of the most common expressions of college seniors everywhere goes something like this: "Now that
I'm near the end of my undergraduate work, I really
feel that I need another year." Just one more year —
new courses could be taken, new books read, more
understanding developed. These prenatal desires expressed by sons and daughters soon to be delivered by
Alma Mater are popularly known to campus counselors
as the senior syndrome. The symptoms commonly take
the form of hesitancy and reluctance, and sometimes
not a little anxiety. To feel comparatively insecure and
uncertain about leaving the womb of the "beloved
mother" is normal and often comes as a surprise to
those anxious seniors who have developed more de-
pendency toward their college than they had realized.

But there is something deeper in this desire for more
time. A need for the fifth year is in reality a way of
referring to the future in general. The fifth year is a

rich symbol of the span of life yet to be lived after the tassel is moved.

I would like to suggest that the fifth year be approached in the spirit of the young couple strolling hand-in-hand along the seashore. As the magic of the moon-lit waters cast its spell upon them, the fellow became so inspired that he burst forth, "Roll on, thou deep and dark blue ocean, roll on!" Not to be outdone, his admiring companion rose to the occasion by responding, "Oh, George, you're wonderful! It's doing it!"

Remember *Ode on a Grecian Urn* by John Keats? Gazing at the silent forms on the side of the urn, the poet saw the small procession making its way out of some little town of long ago to offer a sacrifice. He saw that, but he saw something else and the deeper look moved him to write:

> To what green altar, O mysterious priest,
> Lead'st thou that heifer lowing at the skies,
> And all her silken flanks with garlands drest?

The green altar evokes thoughts of the unspoiled and fresh. It stands in silent rebuke to decay and loss of sense of wonder. The green altar stands for whatever gives basis for hope, adventure, renewal and zest for living. It explains the spirit of Raphael, who was asked, "Which is your greatest painting?" The renowned artist replied, "My next one."

It seems that commencement speakers feel compelled to remind graduates of the fact that commencement means beginning. The tassel-moving experience signifies the old giving way to the new. The term "graduation" suggests renewal, a progressive unfolding of life.

Hopefully the fifth year will witness many commencements in your life.

This is not as easy as it might appear to be, for life has a way of becoming drab and monotonous. Ideals have a way of losing their power to motivate and ennoble. A. J. Cronin's book *The Citadel* describes the erosion of ideals in the life of the main character, a medical doctor. His career began enthusiastically. At first he was deeply committed to serve those who were in need of his training. But gradually his sensitivity to human need waned and his motives lost their quality. His discerning wife, seeing the decay of his once noble spirit said to him, "Don't you remember how you used to talk about life as an attack upon the unknown, an assault uphill, as though you had a castle up there you could see but could not reach?" He responded with a hollow laugh and said, "I was young then, and foolish. That was romantic talk."

Not a few quit sacrificing at the green altar and come to feel the same as Shakespeare's Hamlet who cried:

> O God! God!
> How weary, stale, flat and unprofitable
> Seem to be all the uses of this world!
> Fie on it! Ah fie! 'Tis an unweeded garden,
> That grows to seed.
> — *Hamlet,* Act I, Scene 2

Paul Tournier, the world-famous Christian psychiatrist, believes that peculiar to man is the "great impulse toward adventure" which he considers to be an instinct. In his book, *The Adventure of Living,* he shows how every adventure follows the same pattern and can be described by the same curve. First there is an abrupt ascent — explosive, spontaneous, contagious. Then the joy of discovery becomes reduced to organization and stardardization. What was new and exciting now is routine and dreary. "Adventure ceases," writes Tournier, "as soon as normalcy begins."[1] Thus the need for renewal, to visit life's green altar continues throughout life.

Tournier makes an important distinction between *quality adventure* and *quantity adventure*. The quality adventure is the reach of the spirit for realization of the ultimate experience of value, of quality. The quantity adventure is a compensation for failure to satisfy the soul's quest for God. This shift in adventure leads to a tragic, vicious circle. Money and things become the prize for the person on a quantity adventure. But enough is always a little more than what they have. And so the more quantity is sought, the less it satisfies; and the dissatisfaction increases the quest for more. "A man's life consisteth not in the abundance of the things which he possesseth" (Luke 12:15). Jesus knew that the heart of man can never be satisfied by the kind of life that is lived in terms of physical appetites. "Man shall not live by bread alone." James Terry White points out:

> If thou of fortune be bereft,
> And in thy store there be but left
> Two loaves, sell one and with the dole,
> Buy hyacinths to feed thy soul.

Graduation time should provide the occasion for meditation on what the fifth year would be without the green altar. Someone has well said that "the tragedy of life is not in the fact of death itself. The tragedy of life is in what dies inside a man while he lives -

74

death of genuine feeling, the death of inspired response, the death of the awareness that makes it possible to feel in oneself the pain in the glory of other men."

William James reminds us that whatever is worth possessing must be paid for in daily installments of effort. All of us desire the expanding life. We shrink back from the picture of ourselves growing in years but deteriorating in spirit. We think: "I will keep my mind young and active by reading good books, by cultivating finer tastes in art and music, by nourishing my spirit through worship and meditation." But these worthy intentions are not self-sustaining. Postponement can lay its frosty hand upon them and they can shrivel up and die. "By neglecting the necessity of concrete labor, by sparing ourselves the little daily tax," James warns, "we are positively digging the graves of our higher possibilities."[2]

How quickly the adventurous mind can become the set mind. Nobody wants to be identified with the person whose mind is said to be like cement — thoroughly mixed and permanently set! The father of American psychology shocked the teachers who heard him say, "Old fogyism begins at a younger age than we think. I am almost afraid to say so, but I believe that in the majority of human beings it begins at about twenty-five."[3] James' judgment of several generations ago was recently validated by the findings of a United Press survey. According to this study, the "typical American" is 27 years old and reads less than one book a year. His values are primarily materialistic. He is satisfied with trivial pleasures and is bored with theological matters. He may attend church twenty-seven times a year, but he is indifferent toward the supernatural and spends little time thinking about life after death. Instead of being interested in immortality he absorbs himself principally with football, fishing, and mechanics. Thus the "typical American" evidently finds himself gradually losing through neglect a priceless gift.

> Heaven lies about us in our infancy!
> Shades of the prison-house begin to close
>   Upon the growing boy,
> But he beholds the light, and whence it flows,
>   He sees it in his joy;
> The Youth, who daily farther from the east
> Must travel, still is Nature's priest,
>   And by the vision splendid
>   Is on his way attended;
> At length the man perceives it die away,
> And fade into the light of common day.
> — William Wordsworth in
> *Intimations of Immortality*

One of the most sobering testimonials of the bitter fruits of neglect comes from the following passage in Darwin's brief biography:

> Up to the age of thirty or beyond it, poetry of many kinds gave me great pleasure; and even as a school boy I took intense delight in Shakespeare, especially in the historical plays. I have also said that pictures formerly gave me considerable joy, and music very great delight. But now for many years I cannot endure to read a line of poetry. I have tried lately to read Shakespeare, and found it so intolerably dull that it nauseated me. I have also almost lost my taste for pictures or music. . . . My mind seems to have become a kind of machine for grinding general laws out of large collections of facts; but why this should have caused the atrophy of that part of the brain alone, on which the higher tastes depend, I cannot conceive. . . . If I had to live my life again, ⁻ would have made a rule to read some poetry and li

76

ten to some music at least once every week; for perhaps the parts of my brain now atrophied would thus have been kept alive through use. The loss of these tastes is a loss of happiness, and may possibly be injurious to the intellect, and more probably to the moral character, by enfeebling the emotional part of our nature.[4]

Contrast Darwin's tragic witness with the incident that took place when Solon, the youthful-spirited Greek was traveling in Egypt. After observing him with fascination, an onlooker said, "O Solon! You Greeks are always children. There isn't an old man among you!"

Peter Drucker, perhaps the most respected management consultant in America, expresses the same spirit of our theme. He was not kidding when he said, "Here I am 58, and I still don't know what I am going to do when I grow up."[5]

This quality of youthfulness was once described by the unforgettable and ingenious Walt Disney as "that precious, ageless something in every human being which makes him play with children's toys and laugh at silly things and sing in the bathtub and dream."

Once some startled listeners heard a young Galilean say, "Except ye be converted, and become as little children, ye shall not enter into the kingdom of heaven" (Matt. 18:3). He is our authority for refusing to believe that we inevitably lose our sense of wonder as we get older.

Dr. Frank Crane recognized that

> . . . youth is not a time of life, it is a state of mind. It is not a matter of rosy cheeks, red lips and supple knees; it is a temper of the will, a quality of the imagination. It is the freshness of the deep springs of life . . . You are as young as your faith, as old

77

as your doubt; as young as your self-confidence, as old as your heart; as young as your hope, as old as your despair.

One of the objectives of your college or university should have been to develop in you this growing awareness of the wonders of life. With such growth in knowledge and wisdom should have come a proportionate growth in the ability to get to the green altar. "No matter how learned we are," writes Dr. Ralph Sockman, "the field of knowledge which even the best of us can master is like an island surrounded by a limitless ocean of mystery. And the larger the island of knowledge, the larger the shoreline of wonder."[6]

The journey to the "fifth year" will demand visiting the green altar for continuous rebirth. Samuel Miller, dean of the Harvard Divinity School, describes it in this way:

> For a man's birth is not ended with the first gasps of his breath and the first cry of his lungs. He is born for innumerable births. He is forever pushing his way into new worlds. Through countless experiences by high ecstasies and deep sorrows he plunges to new heights and depths within himself. Through the old symbols and the new insights he sees fresh and alluring vistas. Grief and love lead him far beyond himself. Prophets and poets shout across the ages and call out his soul. Beauty unseals his eyes and reverence leads him to mystery and tenderness. The strange designs of circumstances and purpose, the impact of this world and all its wonders, the dark movings of the inner abyss in himself, all these are avenues of births beyond number.[7]

Rebirth is not an event pinned in by points in time; not an act of the moment. This is not a static experience but one characterized by risk-taking, fresh adventure, goal-setting and goal-reaching, followed by new

78

goal-setting. Thus life offers gateways to everwidening fields and dales, to visions of becoming that can frighten while they thrill, that beckon from distant horizons, that nourish the heart to throb, the pulse to quicken, the heart to respond, the will to prefer. The untraveled road entices because the traveler finds that with each new step, he affirms life with all its mystery and in walking and affirming he comes to understand the glory of continuous rebirth.

The outset of the adventure is always the most difficult stage. Ideas and beliefs change with time and there is a risk in stepping toward the unknown. Beginning again means continual dying of the old self as well as the continual birth of the new self. In this connection, Alan W. Watts' contrast between belief and faith is most helpful. Belief is a firm commitment to what one values. Faith is, according to Alan Watts, "an unreserved opening of the mind to the truth, whatever it may turn out to be. Faith has no preconceptions; it is a plunge into the unknown. Belief clings but faith lets go."

How can we bring to each new day this sense of wonder that combines the familiar with the unfamiliar in such a way that life finds constant renewal? How can we find life's green altar? Again we look to the poet for insight.

> Whether we be young or old
> Our destiny, our being's heart and home,
> Is with infinitude, and only there,
> With hope it is, hope that can never die,
> Effort and expectation, and desire,
> And something evermore about to be.
>
> —William Wordsworth
> *The Prelude*

The green altar is the altar of the Lord. Those who understand kneel there, not asking that life be a peak experience twenty-four hours a day. Neither do they ask for immunity from all that having clay feet means. Rather they request the experience described by the prophet who wrote: "Even the youths shall faint and be weary, and the young men shall utterly fall: But they that wait upon the Lord shall renew their strength; they shall mount up with wings as eagles; they shall run, and not be weary; and they shall walk, and not faint" (Isa. 40:30, 31).

For Green Places

Lord, may there be a still green place
For everyone . . . a little pool
Within a forest where the lace
Of ferns is delicate and cool;
A meadow where across the grass
Small clover-scented breezes pass. . .

And, Lord, if there are those for whom
There is no quiet green retreat,
Oh, let a healing memory bloom
To bring refreshment deep and sweet
And please, Lord, keep it very green
However long the years between.[8]

— Grace Watkins

8

If You Have Promises to Keep

Definitions of the educated person are as many as they are varied. Take this profile for example:

1. "The educated man speaks and writes clearly and precisely.

2. "The educated man has a set of values and the courage to defend them.

3. "The educated man tries to understand his society and how it differs from others.

4. "The educated man looks squarely at the world and its problems — and always with hope."[1]

Or take this definition offered by Dr. Harold Taylor, former president of Sarah Lawrence College, who believes that "the truly educated man is one who has learned to use what he has in ways which are productive both to himself and to his society."[2]

As far as it goes, Dr. Taylor's definition is clear and suggestive, but it lacks that vital dimension that gives the concept of vocation its fullest meaning. He does interpret vocation as a calling, "something to which the individual is drawn by talent and interest," but the Christian concept introduces the reality of the conviction that an individual's life can be employed in accordance with the will of God.

Supposedly, your higher education has provided opportunities and experiences that helped you to develop your talents and to increase your awareness so that you can serve others. If you feel that this was done in response to the Divine will for your life, then you can truly explain work as vocation, as that to which a person is called. It is a high moment when the "hour of knowing" comes as it did to the author of the following:

> Softly I closed the book as in a dream,
> And let its echoes linger to redeem
> Silence with music, darkness with its gleam.
>
> That day I worked no more. I could not bring
> My hands to toil, my thoughts to trafficking.
> A new light shone on every common thing.
>
> Celestial glories streamed before my gaze.
> That day I worked no more; but, to God's praise,
> I shall work better all my other days.[3]
> — Winfred Ernest Garrison

The role of work in modern life takes on new meaning when we realize that most adults spend one-third to one-half of their lives working. This is more time than they devote to any other activity. According to the Bureau of the Census (1968), in 1967 the population of the United States reached and exceeded 200 million people. Of this number those between the ages of 20 and 64 (103 million) comprise the main work force.

Constituting the work force itself were 78 million Americans (49 million men and 29 million women). Three-fourths of these had private employers; one-seventh worked for local, state, or federal governments; and one-ninth were self-employed. The census data further revealed that white-collar professionals, managers, clerks, and salesmen were the largest and fastest growing group, consisting of some 34 million persons.

When the American Institute of Public Opinion made a nationwide survey of workers and their attitudes toward their work, it found that perhaps three out of every five workers hate their work. Some of this frustration and confusion regarding the purpose of work is reflected in the following quotes:

"I go on working for the same reason that a hen goes on laying eggs." — H. L. Mencken

"I like work; it fascinates me. I can sit and look at it for hours." — Jerome K. Jerome

> But till we are built like angels —
>   With hammer and chisel and pen,
> We will work for ourself and a woman,
>   Forever and ever, Amen.
>   — Rudyard Kipling

"Work is something you want to get done; play is something you just like doing." — Harry Leon Wilson

"It is an occupation that illustrates the two tragedies of life: Not getting what you want and getting it." — Oscar Wilde

Contemporary man's attitude toward work has been affected by urbanization, the shift from blue collar to white collar jobs, and a massive movement toward higher levels of education. It is difficult for us to realize the vocational implications of the fact that fifty years ago half of our population lived in small towns or farms, with two-thirds of this group actually on farms. Today only one-third of the people live outside cities and less than 10 per cent are on farms. Expecting this increase in urbanization to continue, demographers are talking about the formation of the megalopolises.

Changes in the educational level of the general population have had important effects on kinds and desirability of work. In 1919, 50 per cent of the adult population had less than eight years of schooling and only 7 per cent had ever been to college. Today approximately half of the adult population have completed high school and almost half of the 18-year-age group are enrolled in college.

An authority in careers and vocations has set forth questions that should be asked by those who are planning their careers: 1) Am I looking for the security of routine work or for challenge — with its attendant penalty for failure? 2) Would I rather be a small cog in a big wheel or visa versa? 3) Should I start at the bottom and work my way up or get on the "aerial trapeze" of a preparatory program in management? 4) Am I happier and more effective as a specialist or a generalist (administrator)? These questions should be answered in terms of your understanding of your interests, abilities and limitations.[4]

A recent shift in the attitude of young people toward value of work is evident. A short time ago a survey by the American Council on Education was conducted among more than 200,000 freshmen. They found that many college students are more concerned about helping others than making money. The top career choice was high school teaching.

Another study conducted during the last half of 1968 showed a great unrest among executives in the 30-to-40-year-old bracket. Although they earned from $20,-000 to $30,000 a year, more than 60 per cent wanted to change jobs. They expressed a preference for smaller companies in which they would have room to grow and have responsibility.

These studies and many others suggest that modern man is involved with finding better ways of developing and fulfilling himself through his work. Ralph Waldo Emerson showed his insight in connection with work and the dignity of man when he gave his famous Phi Beta Kappa address, "The American Scholar," to the Harvard Chapter in 1837. In this speech Emerson declared, "Man is not a farmer, or a professor, or an engineer, but he is all. Man is priest, and scholar, and statesman, and producer, and soldier. In the divided or social state these functions are parceled out to individuals, each of whom aims to do his stint of the joint work. . . .

"The tradesman scarcely ever gives an ideal worth to his work, but is ridden by the routine of his craft and his soul is subject to dollars.

"The priest becomes a form; the attorney a statute book; the mechanic a machine; the sailor a rope of the ship."

A great deal of concern is being expressed by young people of today about the potential of work to provide genuine satisfaction. These satisfactions related to work may be classified as intrinsic and extrinsic. Intrinsic satisfactions are gained from the work itself and meet the worker's needs for self-esteem, personal achievement and fulfillment. Extrinsic satisfactions include money, fringe benefits, and working conditions. These satisfactions are extraneous to the work itself and are commonly taken for granted by those workers having a college level education. Almost every large company admits to losing more than half of the new college graduates in their employ for a period of five years or less.[5]

The other side of the picture also deserves attention. "What would you say are some of the greatest weaknesses of young college graduates who come to you for employment?" This question was asked in a nation-wide Gallup survey of top corporation directors and executives. The answers were summarized as follows:

1. They lack many of the basics of education.
2. They want too much for nothing — all they want is security.
3. They lack drive and ambition; they are afraid of work.
4. They have too much interest in money, fringe benefits.[6]

What is desperately needed in our day is a rediscovery of the sense of vocation. For it is not work per se but the spirit brought to the work which dignifies it and makes it significant. (There is nothing particularly exciting about the estimated more than 1,100,000 dishes that a woman will wash in a lifetime.)

A certain man approached a construction site and noticed three men shoveling dirt out of a long ditch. He walked up to the first man and asked him what he was doing. "Digging a ditch," sneered the worker. Walk-

86

ing on, he came to the second man and asked him the same question. This time the reply was, "I'm making a living." But when he asked the third man what he was doing, a far different answer was given: "Mister," beamed the laborer, "I'm helping to build a cathedral!"

So it is that when our efforts are directly and vitally connected to the goals we value and find attainable, they find strong motivation and deepest meaning. In the opinion of Viktor Frankl, "There is nothing in the world which helps a man surmount his difficulties, survive his disasters, keep him healthy and happy as the knowledge of a life task worthy of his devotion." Meaning given to and derived from work relates directly to our conception of life itself.

Someone has well said, "To love life through labor is to be intimate with life's inmost secret." What is it to love life through labor? A gallant effort to express the answer is contained in the following tribute to a beloved teacher by a grateful student.

What is it to love life through labor?

It is to listen to another's problems with deep interest, understanding, and loving concern.

It is the ability to understand a child's curiosity, and encourage him when those with less perception would restrain his desire.

It is to present oneself to youngsters, unreproachable in language, in thought, and in deed.

It is to plead for a new kindergarten, a library, a better playground, while knowing these things cannot yet be.

It is to unceasingly tell other teachers, "Never give up on a child," and firmly believe that only this is right.

It is to pick up stray tennis shoes, return a lost pencil to its desk, close a forgotten window, or turn off an overlooked record player long after other teachers and children are home.

It is to reveal to every child that which already lies half asleep in the dawning of their knowledge.

It is to walk among the children in the shadows of one's school, not to give of wisdom only, but of faith and lovingness as well.

Finally, it is to know the problems, backgrounds, and lives of thousands of people, and be sincerely interested in each person . . . and most important of all . . .

It is to believe that these people are inherently worth the effort.

What is it to be intimate with life's inmost secret?

It is to charge each child you teach with a breath of this spirit that is in you. As part of this way of life, it is your — and my — responsibility to transmit such a confidence as will create character.

Dr. Elton Trueblood has pled eloquently for an understanding of the principle of vocation. He reminds us that the world is one, both the secular and the sacred, and the chief way to serve the Lord is in our daily work.[7] He deplores the false distinctions too often made in church organizations between the "full-time" work of the minister and the implied "part-time" work of the layman. He suggests that the term "full-life" would be more suitable when used in reference to the Christian's work, no matter what it is.

This exalted conception of the *meaning* of work provides the only lasting motivation needed for *high quality* work. No man's work is menial if it is done in an effort to extend God's purpose in the world. John Gardner said, "We must recognize that there may be excellence or shoddiness in every line of human endeavor. . . . The society which scorns excellence in plumbing because plumbing is a humble activity and tolerates the shoddiness in philosophy because it is an exalted activity will have neither good plumbing nor good philosophy. Neither its pipes nor its theories will hold water."

George Moore wrote a novel in which he told of some Irish peasants in the period of the great depression. In an attempt to provide work for the men who had lost their jobs, the government put them to work building roads. At first the effort appeared to be successful. The men worked well and sang their Irish songs. When they discovered that the roads they were building had no destination but led to dreary bogs and stopped, the men realized that the only meaning in their work was that it provided employment. It was not enough. The men stopped their work and their singing. Explains the author:

> The roads to nowhere are difficult to make. For a man to work well and sing there must be an end in view.

Life's greatest authority taught His disciples to pray for His kingdom to come. Those who pray this prayer have an "end in view." You may remember Tennyson's treatment of the *Odyssey* of Ulysses' visit to a land of enchantment where it was "always afternoon." His poem "The Lotus-Eaters" tells how the sailors found the unusual Lotus plant growing in the land of paradise. After eating the sweet fruit of the Lotus they were content just to sleep and dream and lounge around with half-shut eyes. Here is the way they talked:

> Surely, surely, slumber is more sweet than toil, the shore
> Than labor in the deep mid-ocean, wind and wave and oar;
> O, rest ye, brother mariners, we will not wander more.

Words from Tennyson reveal that he caught a glimpse of God's dream, His divine intention regarding humanity and realized that he could be a participant. He came to know that when we follow Christ

> He wakes desires you never may forget;
> He shows you stars you never saw before;
> He makes you share with Him forevermore
> The burden of the world's divine regret.

There is no more humbling thought than that expressed by St. Augustine: "Without God, we cannot. Without us, God will not." Long ago a person who penetrated the mysteries of life spoke these words: "He that findeth his life shall lose it: and he that loseth his life for my sake shall find it" (Matt. 10:39).

Upon graduation from medical school a young doctor went with the United States Army to Viet Nam in 1954. What he saw during the next two years became indelibly impressed upon his brilliant mind. When his service term came to an end in 1956, he couldn't forget the disease, famine, squalor and suffering that had surrounded him. Somehow the thought of only one fully trained medical doctor for every two million people linked itself inextricably with a sense of mission for his life. Upon his arrival back in America, Dr. Thomas A. Dooley went to the Viet Nam ambassador and volunteered to lead a medical mission to the impoverished little country.

Shortly thereafter, he found out that what he thought had been just a harmless tumor on his chest was malignant cancer. After the operation he dreamed one night of a ceremony that he had seen in the Far East. Every year, before the monsoon rains, the people burne mountain, believing correctly that the ashes fertilized the soil for the planting of the new rice.

In explaining the dream, he said, "I knew the meaning of my dream . . . I must, into the burnt soil of my personal mountain, plant the new seedlings of my life. . . . Whatever time was left, whether it was a year or a decade, would be more than just a duration. I would continue to help the clots and clusters of withered and wretched in Asia to the utmost of my ability."

Recalling the words of Camus, "In the midst of winter, I suddenly found that there was in me an invincible summer," he made his decision to return to Viet Nam. An exhausting twenty-hour-a-day schedule culminated in physical collapse. He was taken back to America where in New York he celebrated his thirty-fourth birthday on January 17, 1961. The next day the world learned the sad news of his death.

How does one explain Dr. Dooley's life of sacrifice and devotion? In an age characterized by an inordinate craze for comfort and convenience, what produces the Tom Dooleys of our time? Perhaps the answer is more than hinted at by the four hauntingly beautiful lines by Robert Frost that Dr. Dooley had inscribed on the back of a medal which he wore around his neck:

> The woods are lovely, dark and deep,
> But I have promises to keep,
> And miles to go before I sleep,
> And miles to go before I sleep.[8]

What makes life worth living and work sacred is 1) having a covenant with God — "promises to keep," and 2) a sense of mission — "miles to go before I sleep."

Any college worthy of the name is unsparing in its

efforts to provide "the habitual vision of greatness." Enough exposure to excellence, coupled with an increasing awareness of individual and social needs, produces in graduates a deep sense of oughtness, of "promises to keep." Convinced of what "ought to be," aware of "what is" and inspired by exposure to great examples, the modern "tassel mover" hopefully looks out at his world and with miles to go before he sleeps prays with the poet, Carl Sandburg:

> Lay me on an anvil, O God.
> Beat me and hammer me into a crowbar.
> Let me pry loose old walls.
> Let me lift and loosen old foundations.[9]

As we bring this little volume to its end, you will have perceived the incompleteness of the journey. Obviously much more could be said. However, if the themes considered have added light, given inspiration and strengthened the lure of the untraveled road I will feel that the purpose of this book has been achieved. Now as you prepare to move into a new stage of life a benediction seems in order, and the one I have chosen is my wish for you:

> The Lord bless you, and keep you:
> the Lord make his face shine upon
> you, and be gracious unto you:
> the Lord lift up his countenance
> upon you, and give you peace.
> — Numbers 6:24-26

Notes

CHAPTER 1

1. The Carnegie Tech Quarterly, quoted by Esther M. Lloyd-Jones and Herman A. Estrin, *The American Student and His College,* (Boston: Houghton Mifflin, 1967), p. 375.
2. J. B. Phillips, *The New Testament in Modern English,* (New York: The Macmillan Company, 1962), I Cor. 13:12, 13. Used with permission.
3. *Time,* Jan. 29, 1965, p. 59.
4. H. F. Lowry, *College Talks,* J. R. Blackwood, ed., (New York: University Press, 1969), p. 111. Used with permission.
5. Ralph W. Sockman, *Now to Live!* (Nashville: Abingdon, 1946), p. 14.

CHAPTER 2

1. Carl Jung, *Modern Man In Search of a Soul,* tr. by W. S. Dill and Cary F. Baynes, (New York: Harcourt), p. 239.
2. Roy L. Aldrich, quoted in *Christianity Today,* May 10, 1968, p. 22.
3. Paper No. I, 1965
4. *Ibid.*
5. "The New Education — Teaching Tomorrow Today," *The General Electric Forum,* Fall, 1966.
6. William S. Sahakian and L. Mabel, *Ideas of the Great Philosophers,* (New York: Barnes and Noble, 1966), p. 27, 28.

7. J. B. Phillips, *The New Testament in Modern English,* (New York: The Macmillan Company, 1962). Luke 11:34-36. Used with permission.
8. "Wanted, A New Pleasure," *Music At Night,* (Garden City, New York: Doubleday), p. 227.

CHAPTER 3

1. Theodor Reik, *Listening With the Third Ear,* (New York: Farrar, Straus, 1948), p. 505.
2. Kahlil Gibran, *The Wanderer,* (New York: Alfred A. Knopf, 1932).
3. Allen Drury, "Mr. Nixon Goes to Washington," *Reader's Digest,* Feb. 1969.
4. Ronald Meredith, *Hurryin' Big for Little Reasons,* (Nashville: Abingdon, 1964), pp. 90-92.
5. Quoted in *Houston Post,* March 8, 1969.

CHAPTER 6

1. Arthur Schlesinger, Jr., "Inability to Cope Root of U.S. Ills," *Houston Chronicle,* Dec. 9, 1967.
2. Eric Fromm, "Age of the 'Mass Man' Is Here," *Houston Chronicle,* Dec. 10, 1967.
3. Marya Mannes, "Needed: Voice of Leadership," *Houston Chronicle,* Dec. 3, 1967.
4. Billy Graham, "American Spirit Hurt by Illusions," *Houston Chronicle,* Dec. 8, 1967.
5. "Is there a Sex Revolution in the U.S.?" 1502 persons aged 21 and older interviewed in over 300 locations across the nation, May 16-19, 1969.

CHAPTER 7

1. Paul Tournier, *The Adventure of Living,* (New York: Harper & Row, 1965), pp. 9, 10.
2. William James, *Talks to Teachers on Psychology and to Students on Some of Life's Ideals,* (New York: W. W. Norton & Co., 1958), p. 62.
3. *Ibid.,* p. 111, 112.

4. *Ibid.,* p. 61.
5. Mary Harrington Hall, "A Conversation With Peter Drucker," *Psychology Today,* Vol. I, (March, 1968), p. 21.
6. Ralph W. Sockman, *Now to Live!* (Nashville: Abingdon, 1946), p. 202.
7. Samuel H. Miller, *The Life of the Soul,* (New York: Harper & Row, 1951), pp. 136, 137.
8. Grace Watkins, "For Green Places," *God's Beautiful World,* (Ideals Publishing Co., 1948).

CHAPTER 8

1. Kirk Grayson, "Four Marks of an Educated Man," in Norman T. Bell and others, *Introduction to College Life: Meanings, Values and Commitments,* (Boston: Houghton Mifflin), pp. 37-44.
2. Harold Taylor, "The American Idea," *op. cit.,* p. 16.
3. Winifred E. Garrison, quoted by T. V. Smith, "Our Reading Heritage," *op. cit.,* p. 131.
4. Peter F. Drucker, "How To Be An Employee," *Psychology Today,* Vol. I, (March, 1968), p. 64.
5. James C. Coleman, *Psychology and Effective Behavior* (Glenview, Illinois: Scott Foresman, 1969), pp. 340, 341.
6. *Houston Post,* May 24, 1967.
7. Elton Trueblood, *The Common Ventures of Life* (New York: Harper & Row, 1949), p. 87.
8. Robert Frost, "Stopping by Woods on a Snowy Evening," in *The Poetry of Robert Frost,* (New York: Holt, Rinehart and Winston, Inc., 1969). Copyright 1923 by Holt, Rinehart and Winston, Inc.; Copyright 1951 by Robert Frost. Reprinted by permission of Holt, Rinehart and Winston, Inc.
9. From "Prayers of Steel" from CORNHUSKERS by Carl Sandburg. Copyright 1918 by Holt, Rinehart and Winston, Inc. Copyright 1946 by Carl Sandburg. Reprinted by permission of Holt, Rinehart and Winston, Inc.

DATE DUE